Reflections on Life

Cover design by Kent Grey-Hesselbein,

KGB Design Studio

Manchester, TN, USA

http://kghdesign.nvaazion.com/

Cover photo by John Nyberg

Reflections on Life

the nostalgic poetry of

Stanley J. St. Clair

Reflections on Life

St. Clair Publications

ISBN 978-0-9801704-1-2

Printed in the United States of America by

St. Clair Publications

P. O. Box 726

Mc Minnville, TN 37111-0726

http://stan.stclair.net

Dedication

This body of work is dedicated to my wonderful wife, Rhonda, who has been a great inspiration to my life and helped me to see more clearly the directions which I should follow. As a result of our relationship and love, my life has become more deeply enriched, and I have become a better and more productive person.

I trust that all who read from these selections will find a reason to laugh, a reason to cry, and will connect in some way to my reflections on the varied experiences which have inspired me to put into words my profound faith in God, my love for family, and my hope for the future.

Stan St. Clair

Table of Contents

Section One:

Meditations

I WAS THERE

I was there when words alone
Caused light to burst from heaven's throne;
And I was there when from the dust
God formed the man who fell to lust.
I was there when wolf and swine
Did board an ark with elk and kine;
And I was there when death and dearth
Of man the deluge gave to earth.
I was there when Sarah laughed,
And Abram lay with Hagar aft.
I was there as from their kin
The eons shaped two lines of men.
I was there in Egypt grand
When Pharaohs paced upon the land;
And I was there through Moses' test
To lead his clan to their bequest.
I was there when Caesars reigned

And from the House of David came

A man of royal birth to teach

Whose message touched the heart of each.

I was there in Mecca mild

The day Amina bore her child;

This father of a different faith

United millions of his race.

I was there in Scotia as

Sinclair and Zeno raised their masts.

And I was there with Christobal

As saying "Land ho" changed it all.

I was on Manhattan's Isle

When towers toppled to but piles,

And cries rang out around the orb

"Oh, peace come soon to hate absorb!"

Who am I? Why, I am Time,

I am History, Myth and Rhyme.

Oh, I am Fact and Fantasy,

I am Agree and Disagree.

(*I was There* was previously published on the *Sinclair Discussion List*, copyright 2002)

I COULD HAVE BEEN

"I could have been," my father said,

"a boxer of some fame.

I shared the trainer of the man

the whole world knew by name.

I knocked him out with one right hook,

he shook and tugged the rope.

'You just don't know your strength, my boy,

you're heavyweight's great hope.'"

"I might have been," he said again,

"a flash upon the screen.

I played a part and did it well,

when I was but nineteen."

"I could have been," my mother mussed,

"secure with Uncle Sam.

The F.B.I. called out to me,

and reached to take my hand.

Who's Who inscribed my name within
a lesser of their books.
A packing firm from old Virgin'
was casting longing looks."

"The ticking of the clock of life,
while classes I would teach,
pushed ever toward a higher goal
my soul did long to reach.
And then your dad," my mother said,
"laid plans like never other,
Allowing me to be his wife,
and thus become your mother."

"*I* could have been a blinding knight,
a scroll clutched in my fist;
a guardian of mysteries
still muddled in the mist.

I could oft walk with noblemen
and claim them as my kin,
but better be a simple man,
my spirit free within.

THE CHOICE

The streaked motley horizon

teased of awakening daybreak;

the moment's intensity immensely surreal.

Yet my cloudy morning mind failed to fully focus.

Before me lay a pressing choice, most crucial.

Not to those of my wretched race

who dashed so gaily through their mundane tasks,

but it to me alone meant life or death.

The final sands of time sifted swiftly downward.

Some action I must risk,

with no delay and no remorse.

And so I did, and here I stand, alone -

fighting the specters of doubt,

grabbing faint glimmers of hope -

but alive I am,

and squarely I will face another day.

(*The Choice* was previously published in *The Colors of Life, the International Library of Poetry,* Watermark Press, Owings Mills, MD, Howard Fly, editor, copyright 2003 by the author)

MOM'S HEART

The year was 'fifty-four,

The sky, October blue.

The house was logs and boards,

But love flowed through and through.

The yard was raked

With piles of leaves,

And pumpkins filled the porch.

The fireplace held a cozy flame,

But Mom's heart held a torch.

The lady was a beam of light,

Wherever she would go.

No need to say Mom was a gem,

To meet her was to know.

(*Mom's Heart* was previously published in *A Proud Heritage, the James Ansel Vinson Family Story*, copyright 1999, St. Clair Publications. Accepted by *Ideals Magazine,* 4-14-2004, suitable for future publication, a division of *Guideposts,* Nashville)

SILENCE

Silently I drove
Sans song or talk.
Oft I'm led to feel,
Silence as an angel
Enfolds me in her wings
And speaks in still impressions
Of heaven's assured protection.

TODAY

Aha! There flies the minstrel

known on earth as Father Time;

the fleeting herald

of that fabled myth

we call tomorrow,

A million yesterdays bygone

he slaughtered dazzling dreams of man

by dole existence

in that solitary state

he termed today.

ONE LAST TIME

There Dad sat with pen in hand
as in the days before the sand
of time eroded youth and will,
and Dad was in the limelight, still.
The grey hair since had crowded out
All but a few dark sprigs about;
disease and grief, like wind and rain,
had caused the man no minor pain.

Determined now, just one last time,
to grace a page with flaming rhyme,
his guitar clutched in his left hand,
with furrowed brow, his right did span
the length and breadth of that blank sheet
until, with masterpiece complete,
the champion of verse and rhyme,
had blessed the world one final time.

One Last Time was written in honor of my father-in-law, Everett Gleeves Prater (1-4-1928 to 11-23-1999), on the day of his funeral, Thanksgiving morning, 11-25-1999.

BEYOND

I have dined with the gentry
and dwelt with the lean;
yet after each plummeting spiral,
the mountaintops still beckon,
the rainbow beyond.

While the mist of sleepy daybreak
sullenly fades,
the popcorn crests of yonder horizon
awaken within me a buoyant spirit,
soliloquizing new ventures waiting.

The prowling path of life
curls ever onward,
mutely awaiting
the unseen stage of abstruse tomorrows
solely revealed to the Ancient of Days.

(*Beyond* was previously published in *Colours of the Heart,* international copyright 2004, Noble House, London, Paris, New York, Nigel Hillary, Poetry Division, UK, slight changes made)

LIFE'S LAMENTATIONS

Time escapes from the flask of Life
like the froth of champagne
at the pop of the cork.

One moment our thirsty lips
are pursed upon Life's sparkling crystal goblet;
then, more swiftly than a tingling mist dissolves
from a silver morn at first ray's peep,
myriad wrinkles have evolved
into a quilt upon our face.

Dawn hath transmuted to dusk.
Where traversed the noon-day fair?
Did we but bat our wistful eyes
to find them laden with cataracts?

And did we boast and realize

That our words were merely gongs?

Oh, Life, where hast thou flown?

POETRY IS

Poetry is

The sound to the unhearing ear,

The sight to the blinded eye,

The light in the darkest night,

The music to one who is mute.

Poetry is

Beauty in an ugly world.

THE ROAD OF LIFE

The trip was long and stodgy,
But it lent me time for thought.
My mind was pensive,
my mind was clear;
The wipers squeaked-
intermittent rain.
The light on the stereo blinked
    as the station faded
    and blended with another.
I tuned out the noises
    one after the other.
I glanced at the clock,
    then back at the road.
I came to a town
    and stopped for the lights.

Signs and buildings,
power poles and lines
zoomed past me.
A century ago my grandfather
was but a tyke.
The interstate I entered
had not been conceived.
The ancestors of my car
were but a dream.
In my life had risen
war and remembrance,
war and regret;
conflicts engulfed in praise,
conflicts barraged with criticism.
The clouds in mingled motion
embraced the roof above
and hid the crests ahead.

Reflections on Life

The endless evergreens which lined
my track brought to mind
the immortality of life.
Kings and kingdoms will vanish
like the fog which dips in the dales.
But the road of life
goes on forever.

QUITE A MAN

Just to meet him you'd never guess.
He was blue-blood on both sides.
He lived a life of sweet frugality.
He never strived for honor,
        though he received it covertly
        from those who knew him well.
All of the glory he'd gladly
        have passed on to the Almighty,
        whom he loved so intensely.
He never ran from arduous tasks;
        nay, he hastened to fulfill them.
His family held the position
        just beneath that of deity.
His mind was mysteriously complex;
        his solid body, brazen brawn.
Quite a man he was, my dad.

(*Quite a Man* was previously electronically published on the *Sinclair Discussion List*, copyright 2004)

ELOISE'S KNOCK

In late September, Seven' five
when at the Gulf, I did arrive;
oh, such a welcome to receive,
the howling knock of Eloise!

A schoolhouse beckoned all about,
in hopes we'd safely sit it out.
An elder gent was led in there
whose heart was failing from the scare.

A nurse was present, God be praised;
with respiration, he was saved.
Miss Eloise soon bade farewell,
and we went home to rest a spell.

MODELS WANTED

Bedazzled by neon,
Enthralled by dreams,
    her mother's pleas
    met deafened pride.

Salty tears foil her face coat;
    a thickened lash
    pulls quite awry.
Her heart in numbness trembles.

Another stranger gleams
    to feel her tender closeness.
She's far from the model
    She was hell-bent to be.

THE VOID

As I gaze soulfully into the void I call my life
the piercing eyes of haunting dreams
yet unfulfilled lurk in the shadows and mock me.
I cannot bear to meet their stares
nor hear the echoing snickers emitting
from the darkened cavern below them.
The forceful brazenness of the man
I once saw in the mirror exists no more.
The fires flamed by the rapid winds of time
have blackened the stalwart wick of my youth.
Suddenly, at the end of the tunnel of darkness
appears a faint hint of hope.
An embryonic flicker grows more vivid.
My strength renews as the forward motion
of my docile limbs gains rhythm
with the livening beat within my breast.
My soul loses sight of all but the light.

In a flash I am at it.

As I plunge into

the now-engulfing incandescence

I become one with it.

My heart spins profusely.

The void dissolved,

the ghost dismissed,

perfect peace prevails.

VAPOR

The days and weeks,
and months and years
on wings of Pegasus fly.
My joys, my hopes,
My doubts, my fears,
Were as a vapor,
Now the sky.

Oh did I vanquish worthy foes?
Perchance I'll linger till they wilt.
My soul in search of sweet repose
lays down its anger with its guilt.

THOUGH MOUNTAINS FELL

The Blue Ridge hold a haunting grasp
upon the hallowed past.
The Cherokee had not a cause
    their treaty they should doubt.
    till murmurings of new-found gold
    like fire were spread about.
Old Hickory sent for Gaines to scout
    and force the natives out.
But he said no,
    and Scott did go
    and formed a Trail of Tears.
    Its memory shall never fade,
    though through a million years
    the mountains fell
    and froze in hell,
    and rivers jelled to jade.

(*Though Mountains Fell* was previously published in *Black Bear*, Blairsville, GA, copyright 2004)

LIFE ON THE FARM

When we lived out on the farm
I thought that we were really poor.
In the meadows grazed our cattle,
and in the barn, the hay we'd store.
The rustic sty was filled with swine,
and goats would dash betwixt our legs.
Chickens roamed about our yard,
and filled their hungry nests with eggs.
Throughout the swamp the berries rambled,
in the fields the corn grew tall.
The garden yielded fresh tomatoes,
potatoes, beans and squash till fall.
Spindly trees would drop their walnuts,
apples, plumbs and grapes were pearls.
The brambles housed the furry rabbits,
And the wooded hills held squirrels.

The mule helped Daddy with the plowing
till the tractor'd finally come.
Our little family worked together
seeing that the chores were done.
Mama sweated cooking victuals;
washing clothes for us to wear,
While Daddy saw that bills were paid,
and that each day was filled with prayer.
Now looking back upon our past,
I know how fully we were blessed.
The fleeting days of life's succession
have veered my views of sweet success.

(*Life on the Farm* was previously published in *A Proud Heritage, the James Ansel Vinson Family Story*, copyright 1999, St. Clair Publications, some changes made)

A CINQUAIN ON LIFE

Life

Too short

Filled with sorrow

Birth, childhood, adulthood, death

Over

Section Two:

Just for Fun

THE CHILD WITHIN

A Calico

was their hero,

she'd grasp her kittens by the nape.

A frog could hide

a prince inside

back when I thought that scotch was tape.

The lone masked man,

with gun in hand,

Sir Lancelot and Guinevere;

each tale was true,

and all brand new,

when double dares would meet no fear.

And even now,

with wrinkled brow,

I feel the breeze beneath my cape;

I'm Superman,

and once again,

I think that scotch is tape.

BOOKS

There are books
    Of every kind
Awaiting looks
    Upon their lines;
Books of birds,
    Of trees and streams;
Books of words
    Of songs and dreams.
Books of truth,
    Books of error;
Books of youth,
    Books of terror.
Books of peace,
    Books of war;
Books so brief,
    And books with more.
Simple stories,

Flaming novels;
Themes of glory,
Tales of bobbles.
Reference books,
Christian endeavor;
Books for cooks,
The wind, the weather.
History past,
Future predictions;
Houses that last,
Political convictions.
Who's the greatest?
What's your sport?
What's the latest
On law or court?
What would you know?
What's your position?
Desire to grow
In your ambition?

Just take a look,

    Begin to read,

For in a book

    Is what you need.

OUR LITTLE NECK OF THE WOODS

When we first settled in these parts

There was no one about,

And we could see for miles around;

The woods were ours to scout.

Then one by one, our fellow man

Was sharing in our dream

To dwell in nature's wondrous land

Of rock and field and stream.

As all good things must fall to fate,

Our time alone, so good,

Has withered into distant past

In our little neck of the woods.

Our Little Neck of the Woods was previously published in *Black Bear*, Blairsville, GA, copyright 2004)

KING ME

"A penny for your thoughts, my son,"

my mother says to me,

while wrapped up in the cares of life

and all its malady.

"My thoughts are worthless, Mother dear,"

I tell her with a smirk,

yet deep inside,

my feelings hide;

my plans are hard at work.

I'll build a castle with a mote,

and servants all about,

I'll snap my fingers and my problems

quickly they'll work out.

I'll mount a steed with lightening speed,

My ducks all in a row.

I'll be the king of everything,

And everyone will know.

BUFF'LO WINGS

When chickens have fingers,
And buff'loes have wings,
Then pigs can fly,
And cows can sing.

And we'll all dine
On shells and pearls,
And girls will be boys,
And boys will be girls.

DÉJÀ VU

I was basked in déjà vu in the gazebo

when a Ford within my view became a repo.

Then my mind all ran amuck,

for I knew that I was stuck

back in the seventies,

on Carson Lane in Reno.

' Came a sound I quite eschew

from a band dubbed Motley Crue,

as I grabbed my nose

to quench the stench of Keno.

(*Déjà vu* was previously published electronically in *The International Library of Poetry*, copyright by the author 2003, poetry.com)

QUIET

Quiet is a mystic state

That's difficult to just locate.

Sometimes it seems you can't get to it

By starting where you are to do it.

From crowded rooms,

Or bustling streets,

Quiet is a fresh retreat.

When your tension's at its peak,

Quiet is the place you'll seek.

Oh, quiet, find me now.

WHOSE FACE?

Whose face is this which stares at me
from yonder mirrored wall?
'Tis far from one I'd hope to greet
as life's swift pages fall.

Whose joints are these which throb with pain
that mine should ne'er have felt?
Whose belly juts beneath my chest
and begs a longer belt?
Whose eyes within my sockets tire
and hunger for repose?
Whose nostrils, filled with stench of death
now throb within my nose?

These legs which drag my form about
are surely not my own;
for mine could jog for endless miles
with not an aching bone.

Whoever pawned this bod' to me
must come and bid it leave
then my old self I'll find once more,
and all my goals achieve.

THE ROLLER COASTER

When I was but a spunky lad
of half a dozen years,
our coach did roll to Myers Lake
for fun, and ne'er for fears.
But there did dwell an awesome beast,
who clasped me in its clutch,
and flung my bony flame about
till I was out of touch
with all reality and rhyme
of life's pretentious game;
it forced me up each rapturous mount,
and harshly down the same.
The shrills emitting from my throat,
I'd never feigned afore,
then followed remnants of the meal
I'd just consumed - and more.
When from the monster's mighty claws,

I finally was ejected,

I thanked my lucky stars I was

in Mother's arms protected.

EBONY EVENING

The ebony evening, a snail as it were,
Came plummeting downward
as thoughts turned to blur.
And ere I could fathom the state of my mind,
There loomed in my visage, macabre, entwined,
Sinews and tissues with fragments of bone,
Then all turned to vapor, and I was alone.

The silence of wailing soon tickled my ears,
But laughter was absent, all riddled with fears.
The air was so thickened, all bloody and red,
Then in rode a horseman in search of his head.
I mustered the courage to wiggle my tongue,
But words were all muted, my pallet was numb.

"Forsooth, forsooth!" the spirit did say,
Then blood turned to curds,

and curds turned to whey.

I realized suddenly I was afloat

In Girnigoe Castle, a lump in my throat.

The message that rang in my head

made me quake,

My clock to my rescue, I soon was awake.

(*Ebony Evening* was previously published electronically on the *Sinclair Discussion List*, copyright 2002)

AUTO-MATION

From rumble seats
to fender skirts
From fender skirts
to fins.
From wide whitewalls
to none at all,
From huge headlamps
to thin.
I'm still amazed
at all the things
They've changed
from end to end –
The modern car
is oh so far
From what they had
back then.

WHEN I SLOW DOWN

When I'm at work, I speed along,
My foot hard on the gas.
I have to make my trips in time,
And many cars I pass.
The scenes around, I hardly see,
The radio's a noise.
The power poles fly by my face,
I wear out cars like toys.
But when I drive on my own time,
I like a slower pace.
It's just surprising what I see
When life's not such a race!
The road becomes a friendly place,
With fields and trees and streams;
In spots it's nice to see myself
Just strolling in my dreams.

Oh, driving can be lots of fun,

Adrift from town to town;

The road is such a nifty place

To be when I slow down

(*When I Slow Down* was previously published in the *Southern Standard,* Mc Minnville, TN. Copyright 1995, minor changes made)

Section Three:

Nature and the Seasons

THE STILL VOICE OF NATURE

The frosty nip of nature was thawing
beneath the nine-o'clock sun.
The transparent smoke guided aloft
by the slow, chilling breeze
dissolved into the grey-blue sky.
The grass was blanched a brownish-green.
All of nature's expanse lay dormant,
And none of her creatures was stirring.
Not a mouse or a squirrel,
Nor even a bird…
Ah! At last a wren!
Yes, a pair of them!
Then all was still, as before.
In muteness creation seemed shouting,
"My time will soon come again!
For I shall rise from the dead,
From the listless face of the earth,

Which yielded all life, even man,

Shall repeat the endless cycle of time

And all shall replenish anew."

(*The Still Voice of Nature* was previously published in *Treasured Poems of America - Summer 1998*, copyright 1998, Sparrowgrass Poetry Forum, Inc., Sistersville, WV)

FEELINGS

Beside the road,

The railroad ran;

Across the heavens,

Clouds did span.

A car sped by,

The sun shone through,

The smell of spring

Made life loom new.

FORWARD

The stirring strains of song
Dance gaily through my brain;
The rhythm of the road hums on along.
I'm mobile once again.

Rough, rounded bales of hay
Are random blurry blobs
About the grassy lea beside the bay,
And Queen Anne's lace dots knobs.

High summer greets my gaze;
The sun of June, my world
Bends brighter to a deeper, haunting phase,
As forward I am hurled.

A WALK IN THE WILD

It seemed that all of Nature
was declaring the radiance of the day.
The lush greenery of the rolling knolls
fused evenly into the distant
peaked horizon, which, in turn,
melted into the rim of the sky.

The intimate cadence of the pileated woodpecker
borrowing his beak beneath
the corky bark of a huge chestnut oak
flooded my senses with
the manna of living.

Above a nearby thicket, a solitary scavenger
circled its skyward borders.

Reflections on Life

The whiff of a wild Rose of Sharon
    wafting on the breeze
    stilled me in my steps.

Slowly, I drew in the sharp mountain air,
    tingling my nostrils;
    enlarging my lungs with freshness of life.

Soon, the gurgle of a rushing brook
    caught my eye to the left.

Kneeling at its side, I received refreshment
    for my thirsting core.

"Why," I probed myself, "am I making this up?
"Why am I not really doing it?
"I will," I decided, "One day very soon."

THE OLD SWIMMING HOLE

The water was cool and so refreshing

Those lively, livid summer days

Down at the old swimming hole.

The years since then have flown so far;

How could it have been so long?

And the miles have separated

My cousins, that place and me.

But in the corner of my mind

Those days still live,

Old Sol still shines,

The water awaits,

And next summer's day, we'll meet once more

To splash in the old swimming hole.

(*The Old Swimming Hole* was previously published in *A Proud Heritage, the James Ansel Vinson Family Story*, copyright 1999, St. Clair Publications)

SUMMER SET

With the dawning of September
There's a shortening of the days,
And the fading sultry evenings
Will be laced with fog and haze.
'Tis the setting of the summer,
Like the setting of the sun:
When the rains call in a cooling,
Then sweet autumn's 'most begun.

THE FOG

Transparent fog is ghastly pale;
a lying quilt about the vale.
As morning sunlight gaily gleams,
the blue field smothered in white streams,
it sparkles on its silvery roof
like neon sequins, so aloof.

THE BLACKBIRDS AND THE FARMERS

When the fall clouds linger
and the leaves turn bright
you can see the flocks of blackbirds
in their migratory flight.

And all around the cornfields,
when the picker's done and gone,
they'll be picking at the nubbins
with their shucks still on.

Although they've tried to kill them
with their poisons and their guns,
the job is just too great a task
to get them every one.

So it seems there is no end now
to this farmers' cornfield plight

of the starlings and the blackbirds

in their migratory flight.

(*The Blackbirds and the Farmers* was previously published in *Happiness Magazine*, Portland, TN, copyright 1983)

THE DIRGE OF EARTH

The dirge of earth reviews its score
of nature's song from years of yore.
The forest hues of mauves and golds
now mutely wave as fall unfolds.

They speak of Summer's sad demise,
and Winter's advent; in the skies
a V formation hovers proudly,
winging southward, honking loudly.

With chilling breath, Sir Autumn smiles,
"I'm visiting for but a while,
my frosty brother, soon you'll greet,
and he'll be nipping at your feet!"

As sure as night replaces day,
much green of earth will fade away.
but on one crisp awakened morn,
the cycle shall be thence reborn.

AUTUMN'S GAIN

The subtle hint of fall

That's creeping through the wood

Make's poplars proudly tall

Find yellow looking good.

As breezes gently puff,

A-drifting in the rain,

When Summer says, "Enough!"

Her loss is Autumn's gain.

(Accepted by *Ideals Magazine* 4-4-2004, suitable for future publication, a division of *Guideposts*, Nashville, TN)

WINTER'S TOLL

When faint footsteps of Fall

Are faded, fully faded,

And Mariah marches

Madly from the pole,

Latch your shaky shutters,

Shadows are a-sinking,

Wiley Winter is a-wandering,

Ripe to claim his toll.

WALKING STICK?

'Tis just a dry and withered stick,
'twas never meant to walk,
upon a grey-aged window sill,
long fallen all its calk.
In the unseen, distant past
this twig grew on a tree;
and these smoky panes were cleaned
by soft hands, tenderly.
Then, within these sullen walls,
this home held hope and love.
Now yesterday has flown to mist,
as an illusion's vanished dove.

Section Four:

Faith and Love

SHADES OF GREY

For everyone, a part of life is lived in
shades of grey.
We try to justify faults by saying,
"What the hey?"
The problem with the color grey is
how that it's composed.
Our lives start like a tender bud,
a purest blanca rose.
Life's faintest breeze, the dust puffs up,
to taint the blossoms fair.
The gardener who first planted us,
provided for our care.
He sent his Son into our world
to wash away the grey,
And those cleansed by His crimson stream
will bloom with Him some day.

(*Shades of Grey* was previously published in *The International Who's Who in Poetry*, copyright 2004 by *The International Library of Poetry*, Watermark Press, Owings Mills, MD)

PRESS ON

Evil's army marches onward;

Sin is flanked by Death,

Heaven's omnipotent host undaunted

Hears ahead the victory song.

The scroll was sealed, fixed and certain,

Press on, infinity, press on.

THE VINE

Up the wall there grows a vine
Until the end of space and time.
Out the window flows the smoke,
So only soot is left behind.

Out the window stares the girl
Whose charcoal hair is filled with curl,
And the thoughts that press her mind,
I can't read 'cause I'm too blind
To read the thoughts within her heart,
Which I pray doth beat for me,
That together we would be

Till the vine no longer grows
Up the wall on which it goes,
And the smoke no longer swirls
Through rock chimneys o're the world,

Yes, together we would be

Throughout eternity -

Up the wall there grows a vine.

(*The Vine* was previously published in *Enchanted Dreams*, copyright 1998, The Poetry Guild, Bath, OH)

IF I COULD CAPTURE

If I could only capture
    The glory of the rainbow,
The beams of streaming sunlight
    Bursting from the breaking clouds;
The joy of a first-time mother
    As she holds her newborn to her breast…
The beauty of his beloved
    In the eyes of a shy young lover;
The unbridled power
    Of the rushing Niagara;
The faith of a father
    In his namesake son…
The love for their flag
    In the tattered troops
    On the shores of Iwo Jima;

The pride of a bride

As she whispers, "I do"...

If I could but harness

The sum of all these mysteries

And encase them in a frame

For all the world to view,

And if we could perceive

The force of their dominion,

Even then, we'd not begin

To catch a glimpse of God's passion

For His children.

(*If I Could Capture* was previously published in *From the Pens of His Sheep*, copyright 1999, Sunset Hills Church, Mc Minnville, TN, some changes made)

THE ENDS OF THE STREAM

I used to deem it fun

To roll with the flow.

But one day I discovered

I was headed downstream

To the hungry mouth

Of an ocean filled with salt.

My destination was a place

Where water was all

That the eye could see.

But those who drifted there

Would drown for want

Of a single drink.

Then I scraped the courage

To paddle up the stream.

At times my trip

Has not been easy,

For I have found myself

At constant war

With the raging rapids of life.

But somehow the battle

Seems to be worth it all

When I think

Of the end of the journey;

For there lies a clear, gelid spring;

The source of life eternal.

(*The Ends of the Stream* was previously published in *From the Pens of His Sheep*, copyright 1999, Sunset Hills Church, Mc Minnville, TN)

THE CRY

In depth of night, I heard a cry
I could not understand.
I tried to find from whence it came,
But saw no beast nor man.

I went to bed and tried to sleep,
But then it came again,
And so I reckoned it to be
A lonely wailing wind.

But then once more, a third loud cry
Now seemed more like a voice,
And thus I focused all my mind:
I felt I had no choice.

"Help!" was the word I knew I heard,
Which echoed through the night;

The chilling sound, which rang through town,
Must be a child in fright!

So I arose, with light in hand,
And searched from here to there;
In spite of all, I searched in vain,
No one was anywhere.

Although the cry was silent now,
I rested nary more.
Then just last night, in soulful sleep,
I dreamt that at the door

A knock came soft, and when I went,
There stood a bearded man.
He stared at me with eyes aglow
And reached out for my hand.

"Do you know me?" the Lord did ask,

"You've sought help in the past.

Then one dark night I cried to you

To others help, at last."

IF I LOVE

If I love,

I will not lean.

If I love,

I will not use.

If I love,

I will but give.

If I love,

I will, myself, be used.

GOD WANTS

God wants my love

much more than my money;

He wants my thoughts

much more than my pledge.

Heaven can wait

for small sacrifices -

True service comes

from the heart, not the head.

LOVE REVEALED

I gazed into her limpid eyes

And what there did I see?

Her tears had washed away disguise,

Revealing love for me.

A climbing rose,

A clinging vine,

A thread entwines

Her heart with mine.

MAJESTY

There's majesty in mountains,
the valleys and the sky;
there's majesty in oceans
that never shall run dry.

There's majesty in caverns,
in cliffs and rocks and trees;
There's majesty in starry nights,
and all that man can see.

There's majesty in elephants,
and in the small ameba;
There's majesty in tall giraffes,
and in the striped zebra.

In everything that God has made,
His fingerprints are found,

And "majesty" is just a way

to say God's still around.

REFLECTIONS ON LIFE

You used to think I hung the moon.

But I didn't.

You felt in your love for me

that the endless universe

revolved around me.

But it doesn't.

Your sun rose and set in me.

but your sun proved only to be

a blind mirage on a desert

of endless regret.

Ambivalent emotions tumbled

the steaming castles you had

sought ahead in the sand.

Your soul had only to grip

the reality that your hopes

and desires were built

of the dust of the earth.

That I, yes even I,
was a mere bit of crumbling clay,
a particle of imperfect humanity.

Then, lying upon the parching patio,
near the entrance to eternity,
as your blistered tongue withdrew,
and begged you for a consummation
to your pain,
your glazing eyes caught the form
of a peaceful shepherd.
Unwilling to trust in a final false hope,
you pivoted your head.
But again your mind registered
the evidence of His presence
through the gate of your ear
as He whispered your name.
He lifted your slumping torso
and pressed a vile to your lips.

Hungrily you guzzled
the liquid of life
till newness invaded your soul.
It seems that eons have elapsed
since I last laid eyes upon you.
I would not accept your passionate plea
to seek the stranger.

Father Time had left no scars upon me,
and Lady Luck danced gaily
at my side.
But alas, I who knew no want,
am but a glimmer of my former self.
The frolicking freedom of youth
has gone to indwell another.

Disease and Distress
are my jabbering companions.
Their gnarled fingers rip out my heart.

Oh that I had headed,

but I did not.

How I wish that someone could find me

and point me to this Master of Life.

But I know not where the River of Destiny

has taken you,

nor how to find Him on my own.

Please help me,

oh, Spirit of Hope!

If you detect the cry

of my fading heart come to my aid,

for I am lower than the abyss,

and my limp life seeps away.

Those eyes!

I have never seen such love!

Take me and enfold me in your bosom!

Such peace…such…

THE SEARCH

So quarrelsome and weary-worn,
And somberly aloof;
He fingered through the volumes as
He ambled toward the truth.

The tangled tide of evening had
Long mingled with the morn;
He lingered on the legends while
He tossed away the porn.

He searched for only nuggets which
The fire could melt to gold;
And labored o're the mythic mounds
Which Greed had bought and sold.

His eyes so harshly haggard and
His brain so badly burned;

A voice innate within him spoke

A spark which he had learned

At the apron of his mentor as

A wee and wonton waif,

"The Spirit from above you

Will in Truth your heart keep safe."

THIS WORD CALLED LOVE

A magic word was adrift in the air:
A tiny sound on the tip of each tongue.
If only one could grasp its definition
The finger of fate could point to peace.

I sat in schools of higher learning
In search of this special world called "love".
But there, I noted it not.

Someone said that in a singles' bar
I could end my passionate quest.
But there, each eye was ever eager,
And none had found the way.

I asked a traveler, who told me clearly,
"Go to the tropical islands,
There you'll find sure love."

So off I journeyed upon a vessel
Across the deepest blue;
But there, alas, again,
Though pleasure seemed abounding,
It all left emptiness.

The time flew past, and then I thought,
There is no reality to this fabled fantasy.

But then one morn, in a simple chapel,
Invited by a stranger,
I met a lovely maiden
With eyes of purest peace.

I knew that she,
This unlikely lass,
Had found that unique feeling.

And since that very day,

The love that I have known

Came not from mortal man,

For God above gave me this love;

It is He alone who can.

A NEW TOMORROW

Our globe grows warm when Sol is shining;

Doom doth dawn when skies turn grey.

Invert, oh frown of peace declining,

Wither up and flit away.

Proclaim, oh world, a new tomorrow,

Lit by heaven's fondest star.

With myth and mayhem banned in sorrow,

Love and peace be all that are.

WITHOUT

Without a war no foe is slain,

Without some pain we have no gain.

Without remorse there is no peace,

Without confession, no release.

NEW, FRESH, CLEAN

Today is brand new, and it's quite unique;
It's not just a slice of yesterday's pie.
Yesterday's gone with all of its failures;
Past glories are now just a gleam in the eye.

Today is tomorrow we spoke about yesterday;
All of our dreams we'd finally fulfill.
Today is a rosebud just waiting to open;
A trickle of water, just waiting to spill.

Today is as fresh as its first cup of coffee;
Naïve to the world like a baby's first cry.
Today is to mankind as a slate that is empty
Awaiting the sprawls from the chalk nearest by.

Today is still clean so why make it skuzzy
By tracing the paths which failed in the past?

Today, my dear friend, shall be what you make it,

So blaze a fresh path to triumph at last.

PSALM 100

Shout to the Lord, oh fullness of earth;
Worship the Lord with gladness and mirth.
Come before Him with joy in your song;
Know that the Lord our God is so strong.
Make us, He did, to Him we must yield;
We are His fold, the sheep of His field.
Enter His gates with much thanksgiving;
Enter His courts with praise for living;
Give Him all glory, laud His great name!
God is so good, and ever the same.

PROVERBIAL MYSTERIES

There are three things amazing me;

Four things I do not understand:

the way a ship sails on the sea,

the way a maiden loves a man,

the way an eagle soars and glides,

the way a snake on rocks can hide.

WHEN GRANDMA WENT

When Grandma went to meet the Lord,
I had but seven years.
My father at her side had stayed
with mix of smiles and tears.

Her lids had widened to a glare;
Her simper broadened to a grin,
"Look at those shiny men," she said,
then slumped upon her bed again.

That night she passed; he'd gone to rest,
but wakened from his sleep;
a voice so clear spoke to his soul,
"Your mother's home with me."

ON SHORTNESS OF LIFE

Our days pass by as a mist dissolves
into the balmy fragrance of a summer's morn.
A life is barely blossomed till winter's
fluffy flakes light about the temples.
An etching on the wall pronounces love.
The name would not be known a mere breath ago.
A new baby's lungs burst forth
their welcome to the world.
Where may the dreams be found
which flooded the mind of yesterday?
A large earthmover breaks the virgin soil,
and drives the farm further from the city.
What is progress and what is life?
Where may truth be known?
Only in eternal love may happiness be found.
Nothing less - nothing more.
The beginning and the end.

THE PARADOX OF LIFE

Out with the new, in with the old;
The paradox of life;
To watch the young man metamorphose,
As mirrors lurk about.
Sparse argent hues upon the roof
Supersede the raven rich.

The midriff expands,
The memory declines
As swiftly shadows shorten –
The paradox of flimsy, shallow life.

Then a hidden door cracks but a mite
And mystic hope puffs in.
A dimming candle flame renews;
Fresh light un-blossoms a ghost;
The spirit of bygone ambition

Turns back a page.

Today becomes yesterday.

The paradox of life.

THE LION AND THE LAMB

While mingling and mangling
Toward Knickety-Knack
    amidst the dunes of sand
    a thunderous roar shook
    slumbering stock:
    the lion addressed the lamb.

"If swords shall plowshares truly be,
    and pruning hooks
    from spears evolve,
    then Knickety-Knack
    must veer her plea,
    and Pharaoh's gold dissolve."

The lion stooped to be the lamb,
    and glory enveloped Zion,
    then through the blood,

and through the flame,

the lamb became the lion.

www.ingramcontent.com/pod-product-compliance
Lightning Source LLC
LaVergne TN
LVHW091010080826
845145LV00003B/1202